# Don't Forget Us, Little Bear

Written by
Haiying Wu

Translation by
Charles Nichols

Illustrated by
Chen Li

SEAFLAME
Children's Books

A gray rabbit lived on the north side of the grassy field. A white rabbit lived on the south side. They were both good friends with a little bear.

"It's time for me to hibernate for the winter. I won't be able to come play with you anymore." The bear felt winter had come much too soon.

"Will it be for very long?" The gray rabbit ate a berry.

"You won't forget about us, will you?" The white rabbit ate a berry too.

"It will take all winter, but I won't forget you." Although the bear said this, the rabbits were still worried.

The gray rabbit felt that after a long time, everyone forgets things. "I can't remember which flowers bloomed last spring."

The white rabbit also felt the bear's memory was not so good. "You forgot about the three river stones I had."

"I don't want to forget you. But I have to hibernate." The little bear thought long and hard, but couldn't come up with a solution. What could he do to remember?

"We'll go visit you every day. That way you won't forget us." The gray rabbit finally came up with an idea.

"But my eyes are closed while I'm hibernating. I won't be able to see you."

"We can visit you in your dreams." The white rabbit was quite pleased with his plan, but how would they enter the bear's dreams?

The rabbits couldn't figure it out, so they went to ask their wise friend, old owl. The owl blinked his big eyes and said to them very seriously: "The little bear hibernates to avoid the cold, so warm things will surely get into his dreams."

"The sun is very warm!" The gray rabbit immediately thought.

Old owl reminded the gray rabbit: "Let sunlight into the bear's dreams? Then he will only remember the sun."

"To stay warm in the winter, we grow a thick fur coat and shed our light summer fur." The white rabbit was correct. "We can share some of our warmth with the bear."

The old owl also reminded the white rabbit: "Your fur will fly everywhere and won't keep him warm."

How could they give the bear warmth he could hold on to?

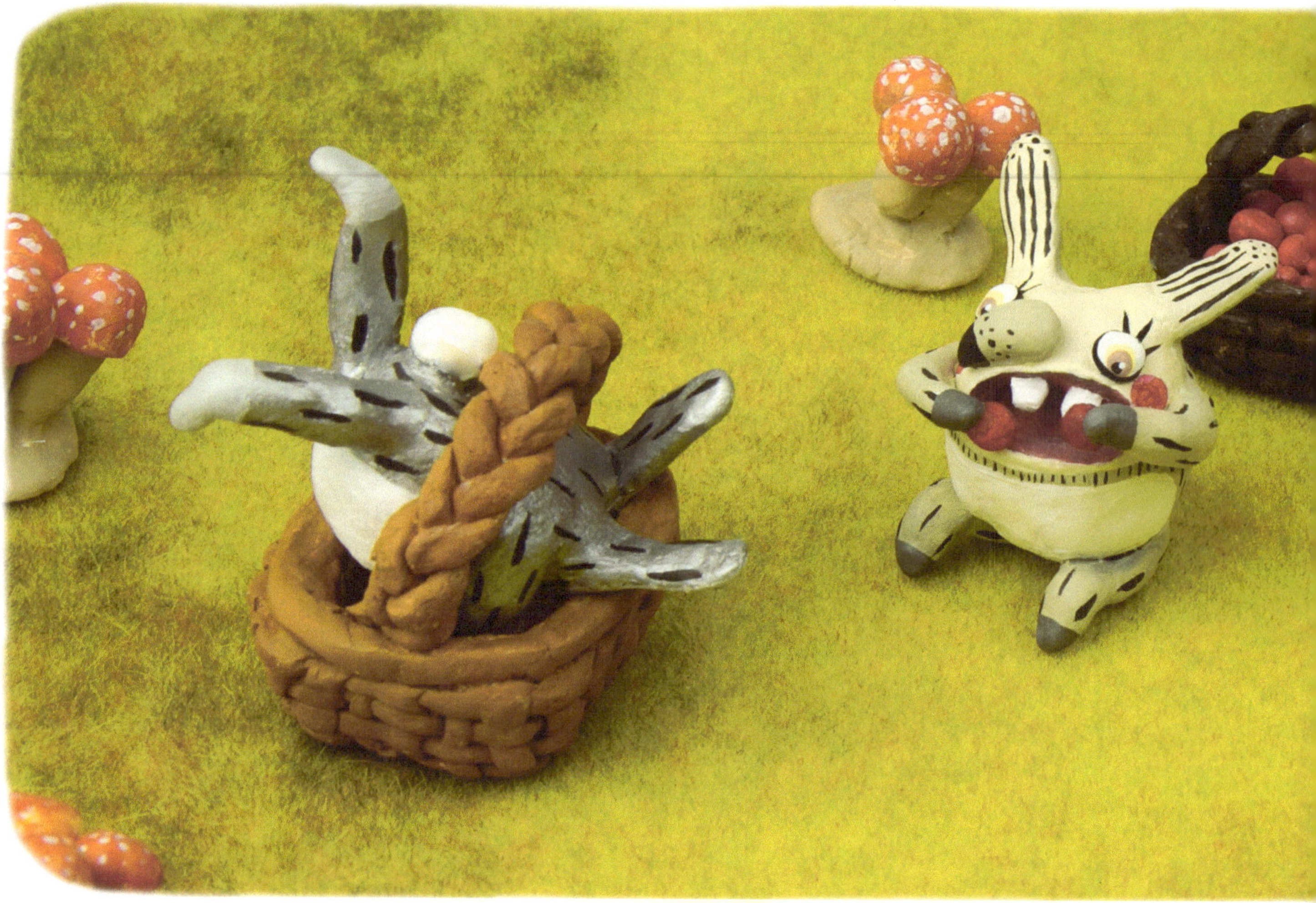

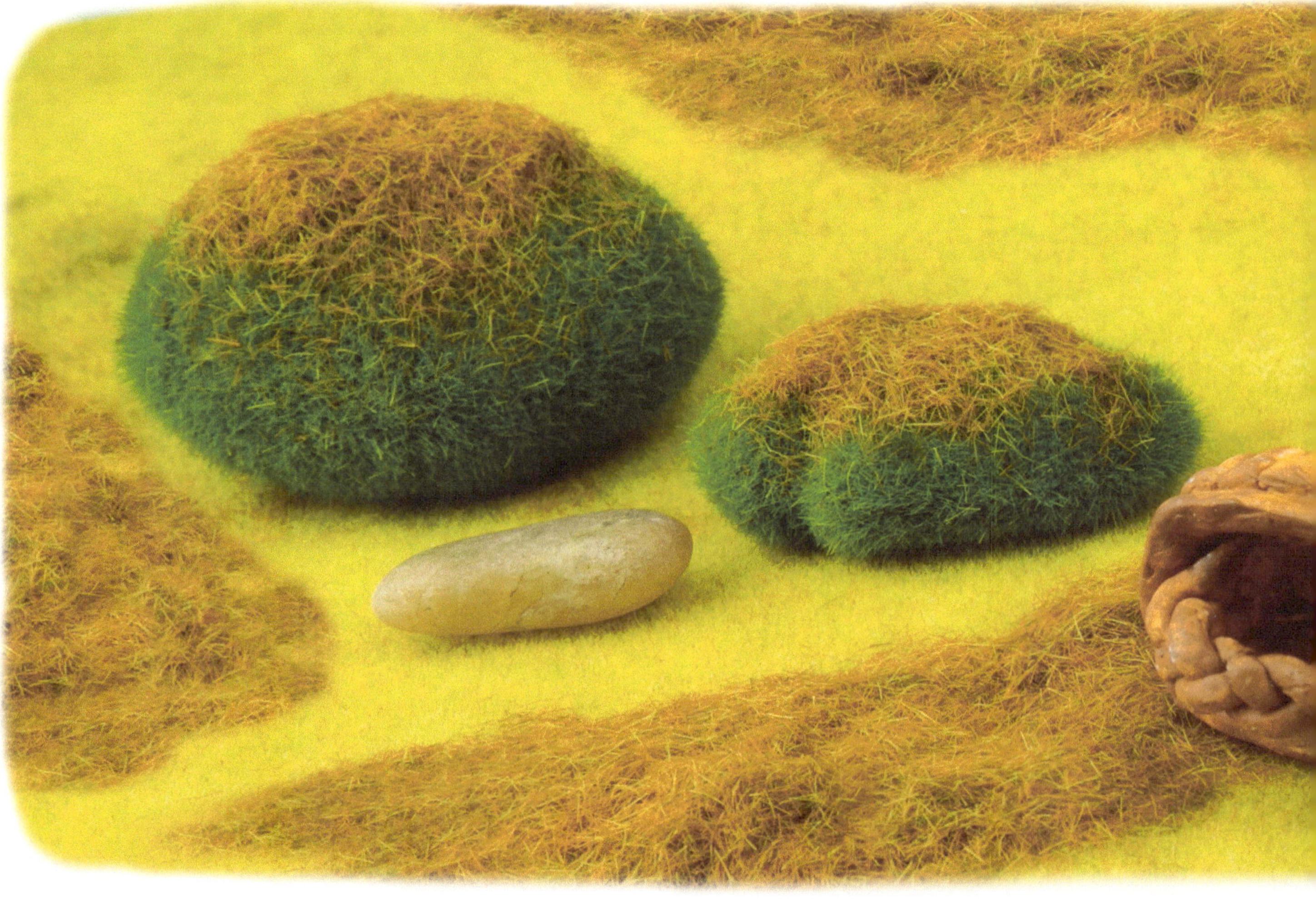

While the rabbits tried to think of a solution, a gust of wind knocked the baskets of berries over, sending the straw lining flying out.

"Straw will get blown away, but a basket made from straw won't." The gray rabbit thought up a clever idea. "We can weave our fur together and give it to the little bear!"

"The little bear is the best at basket-weaving. He must be able to weave a blanket too." The white rabbit also had a clever idea.

The gray rabbit carried his basket on his head. The white rabbit dragged his behind him. They ran back home to collect all their shed fur.

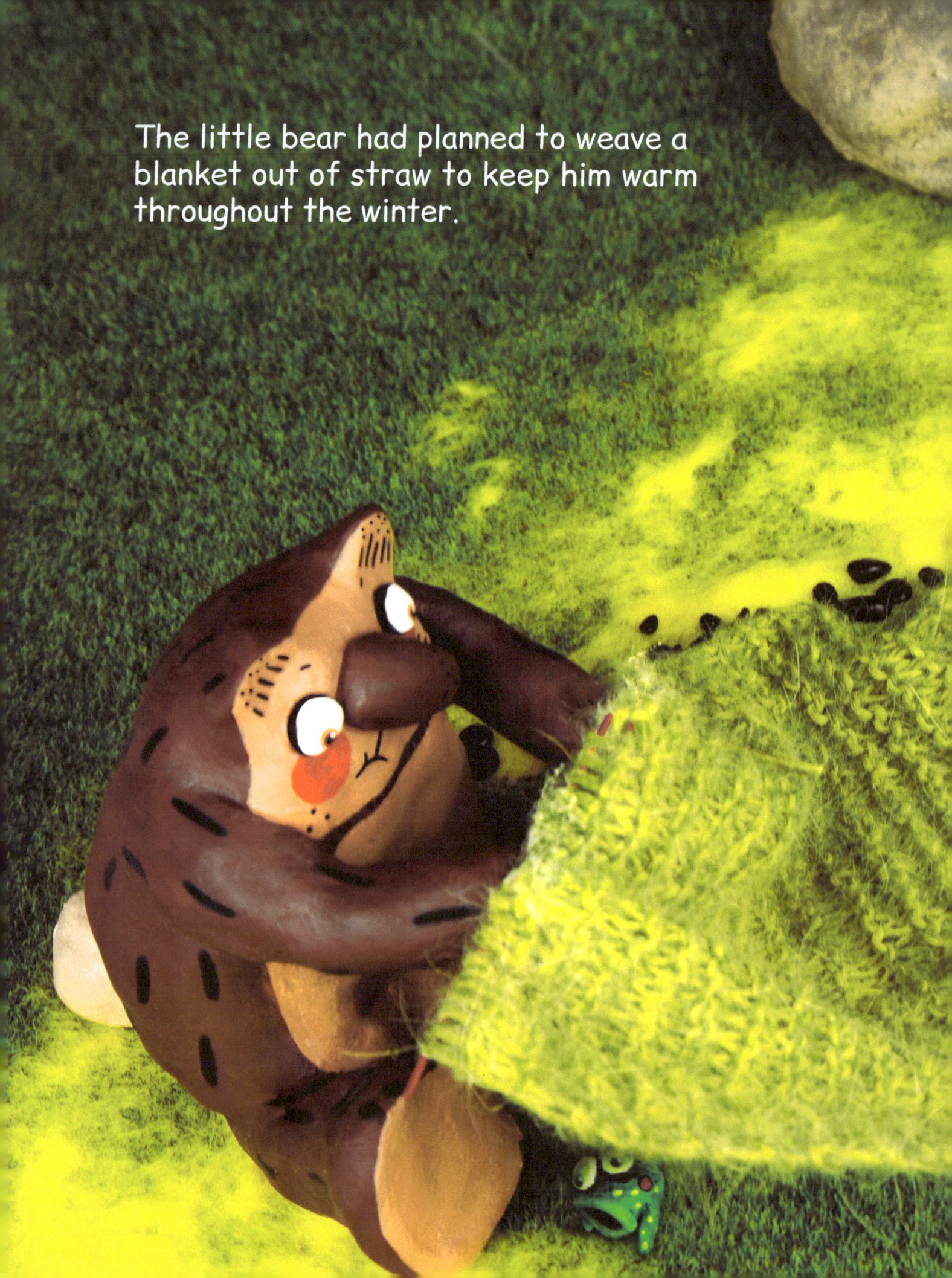
The little bear had planned to weave a blanket out of straw to keep him warm throughout the winter.

Instead, he used the rabbits' fur to weave a softer blanket, and it kept him even warmer throughout the winter.

All through the winter, the little bear slept with a gray-and-white checkered fur blanket. It was just like the rabbits were there with him. Even his dreams were warm and comfy.

**Haiying Wu** is an award-winning author of several popular children's books. Her picture book series *Wow! The Classic of Mountains and Seas* was selected for the 2020 Motion Force China Original Animation Publishing Support Program, and her book *Grandpa Likes to Hide and Seek* won the 2017 Hsin Yi Picture Book Award. She lives in Tangshan, China and Toronto, Canada.

**Charles Nichols** was born in Houston, Texas in 2004 and has lived in Calgary, Alberta since 2012. He has been offered admission to the University of Toronto Faculty of Arts & Science. He has long had an interest in creative writing, aspiring to have a career as a novelist.

**Chen Li** born in 1989, is from Jingzhou, Hubei, China. She received her BFA degree in visual communication from the Hubei Institute of Fine Arts and an MA degree from the Birmingham City University of also in visual communication. She engaged in program post-production and editing at the Hubei TV station, China from 2013 to 2015. Currently, she is settling in Canada and engaging in children's book writing, illustrations, and children's painting education. Two of her works 'Memory' and 'Dream' were selected for the 10th Annual President's Art, Craft, and Design Exhibition in Calgary, Canada 2020.

DON'T FORGET US, LITTLE BEAR

Text copyright © 2021 by Haiying Wu
Illustrations copyright © 2021 by Chen Li
All rights reserved, including the right of reproduction in whole or in part in any form.

English Translation by Charles Nichols
English edition edited by Haibo Xu

Chinese edition published under the title 留住小熊的记忆 by China Light Industry Press Ltd in 2022.

English translation edition published by Seaflame Children's Books with the express permission of China Light Industry Press Ltd.

The text for this book was set in Comic Relief and Source Han Serif. The illustrations for this book were created using clay, photography and digital techniques.

Identifies:
ISBN 978-1-7782214-3-9 (eBook)
ISBN 978-1-7782214-4-6 (Paperback)
ISBN 978-1-7782214-5-3 (Hardcover)

www.ingramcontent.com/pod-product-compliance
Lightning Source LLC
Chambersburg PA
CBHW041709160426
43209CB00017B/1782